Deleted
W9-AET-627

Deleted

Pebble Plus

LET'S LOOK AT COUNTRIES

# LET'S LOOK AT SOUTH AFRICA

BY NIKKI BRUNO CLAPPER

CAPSTONE PRESS
a capstone imprint

Pebble Plus is published by Capstone Press,
1710 Roe Crest Drive, North Mankato, Minnesota 56003
www.mycapstone.com

Copyright © 2018 by Capstone Press, a Capstone imprint. All rights reserved. No part of this publication may be reproduced in whole or in part, or stored in a retrieval system, or transmitted in any form or by any means, electronic, mechanical, photocopying, recording, or otherwise, without written permission of the publisher.

**Library of Congress Cataloging-in-Publication Data**
Names: Clapper, Nikki Bruno, author.
Title: Let's look at South Africa / by Nikki Bruno Clapper.
Description: North Mankato, Minnesota : Capstone Press, [2018] | Series: Pebble plus. Let's look at countries | Includes bibliographical references and index. | Audience: Ages 4-8.
Identifiers: LCCN 2017037877 (print) | LCCN 2017038536 (ebook) | ISBN 9781515799283 (eBook PDF) | ISBN 9781515799160 (hardcover) | ISBN 9781515799221 (pbk.)
Subjects: LCSH: South Africa--Juvenile literature.
Classification: LCC DT1719 (ebook) | LCC DT1719 .C55 2018 2018 (print) | DDC 968--dc23
LC record available at https://lccn.loc.gov/2017037877

**Editorial Credits**
Juliette Peters, designer; Tracy Cummins, media researcher; Laura Manthe, production specialist

**Photo Credits**
Getty Images: Francois Nel, 16; iStockphoto: Henrique NDR Martins, 13, ManoAfrica, 1; Shutterstock: Andrea Willmore, 22-23, 24, bonchan, 19, Denis Mironov, 21, elleon, 9, Francesco Dazzi, 5, Garth Fuchs, Cover Top, Globe Turner, 22 Top, Hedrus, 11, JMx Images, 10, Linda Nienaber, Cover Bottom, Cover Back, Mai Groves, 17, Monkey Business Images, 15, nale, 4, Olaf Holland, 3, Richard van der Spuy, 6-7, Utopia_88, Cover Middle

## Note to Parents and Teachers

The Let's Look at Countries set supports national curriculum standards for social studies related to people, places, and culture. This book describes and illustrates South Africa. The images support early readers in understanding the text. The repetition of words and phrases helps early readers learn new words. This book also introduces early readers to subject-specific vocabulary words, which are defined in the Glossary section. Early readers may need assistance to read some words and to use the Table of Contents, Glossary, Read More, Internet Sites, Critical Thinking Questions, and Index sections of the book.

Printed in the United States of America.
010774S18

R0452497736

# TABLE OF CONTENTS

Where Is South Africa? . . . . . .4
From Grasslands to Mountains . . .6
In the Wild . . . . . .10
People . . . . . .12
On the Job . . . . . .14
On the Field . . . . . .16
At the Table . . . . . .18
Famous Site . . . . . .20

Quick South Africa Facts . . . . . 22
Glossary . . . . . 22
Read More . . . . . 23
Internet Sites . . . . . 23
Critical Thinking Questions . . . . . 24
Index . . . . . 24

# Where Is South Africa?

South Africa is a country at the southern tip of Africa. Its capitals are Pretoria, Cape Town, and Bloemfontein.

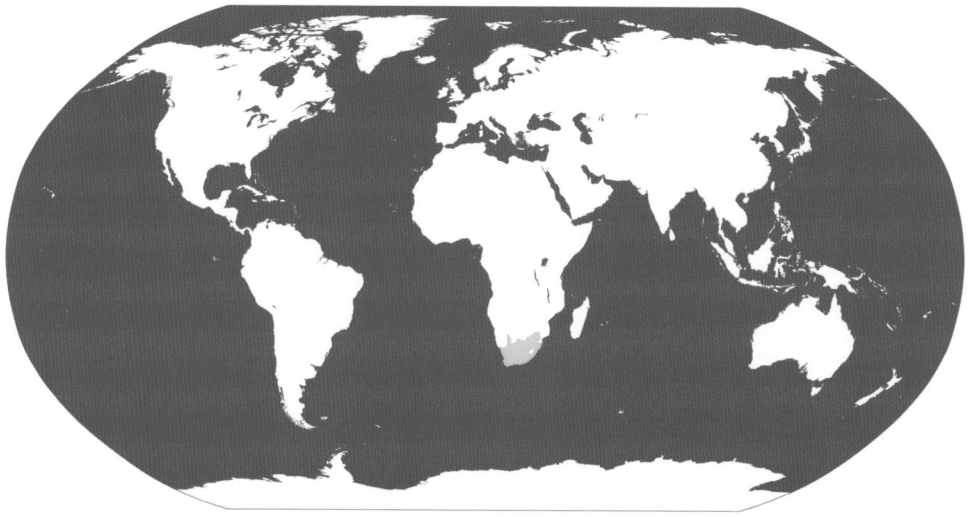

South Africa

## From Grasslands to Mountains

Much of South Africa's land is a plateau covered in grasslands. The climate is dry. Droughts are common.

Mountain ranges surround
the grasslands in a U shape.
The most famous range
is called the Drakensberg.
This means "Dragon's Mountain."

# In the Wild

Leopards, cheetahs, and lions live in the grasslands. They hunt zebras, wildebeest, and antelope. Penguins live along the coast.

zebras

# People

South Africa's people have many different backgrounds. Most people are black. Others are white, Asian, or mixed race.

# On the Job

Some South Africans work in gold mines. Others build cars or make clothes in factories. Tourism jobs are common.

# On the Field

Many South Africans love sports. Rugby, boxing, and running are popular. Athletes climb, bike, and hike in the mountains.

rugby

# At the Table

South Africans eat a lot of meat. The meat is often barbecued or dried. Bobotie has baked meat mixed with egg and fruit.

bobotie

# Famous Site

Table Mountain towers over the city of Cape Town. The mountain has a flat top. People climb it on foot or in a cable car.

# QUICK SOUTH AFRICA FACTS

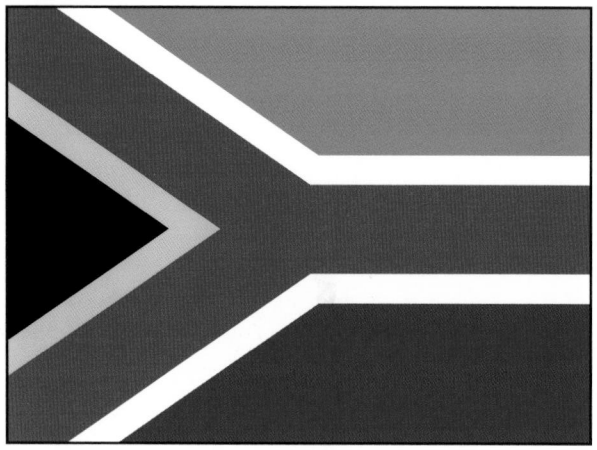

South African flag

**Name:** Republic of South Africa

**Capitals:** Pretoria, Cape Town, Bloemfontein

**Other major cities:** Johannesburg, Durban

**Population:** 54,300,704 (July 2016 estimate)

**Size:** 470,693 square miles (1,219,090 sq km)

**Languages:** isiZulu, isiXhosa, Afrikaans, English, isiNdebele, SeSotho, Sesotho sa Leboa, SiSwati, Xitsonga, Setswana, Tshivenda

**Money:** rand

# GLOSSARY

background—information that helps describe a person, such as race, education level, and religion

cable car—a car pulled by an overhead or underground cable

capital—the city in a country where the government is based

climate—average weather of a place throughout the year

drought—when the land is dry because of too little rain

mine—a place where workers dig up minerals that are underground

plateau—an area of high, flat land

tourism—the business of taking care of visitors to a country or place

# READ MORE

**Aloian, Molly.** *Cultural Traditions in South Africa.* Cultural Traditions in My World. New York: Crabtree Publishing Company, 2014.

**Perkins, Chloe.** *Living in . . . South Africa.* Living in . . . New York: Simon Spotlight, 2016.

**Shoup, Kate.** *South Africa.* New York: Cavendish Square Publishing, 2018.

# INTERNET SITES

Use FactHound to find Internet sites related to this book.

Visit *www.facthound.com*

Just type 9781515799160 and go.

# CRITICAL THINKING QUESTIONS

1. What are some sports and activities South Africans enjoy?
2. What is a capital?
3. How can people get to the top of Table Mountain?

# INDEX


antelope, 10
Bloemfontein, 4
Cape Town, 4
cheetahs, 10
climate, 6
Drakensberg, 8
droughts, 6
food, 18
grasslands, 6, 8, 10
jobs, 14
leopards, 10
mountains, 8, 16, 20
penguins, 10
plateau, 6
Pretoria, 4
sports, 16
wildebeest, 10
zebras, 10